30p

D0296429

North
TYNESIDE
Libraries & Arts Department

∫

FABLES FROM AESOP

FABLES FROM

ILLUSTRATED BY
MAURICE WILSON
BLACKIE OF
LONDON AND GLASGOW

AESOP

RETOLD BY JAMES REEVES

ISBN 0 216 90428 5 (CASED)
ISBN 0 216 90429 3 (PAPER)

BLACKIE AND SON LTD.
BISHOPBRIGGS, GLASGOW G64 2NZ
450/452 EDGWARE ROAD, LONDON W2 1EG

PRINTED IN GREAT BRITAIN BY R. & R. CLARK, EDINBURGH

CONTENTS

INTRODUCTION

Nobody knows for certain who made up Aesop's Fables. Whether there ever lived, as we are told, a slave in Greece with the name of Aesop, we shall never know. It seems probable that such a man did exist two thousand five hundred years ago, and that he gained a reputation as a teller of fables. These were so popular that they circulated widely, and many were added which were certainly not the work of Aesop. There are other legends about this remarkable slave: some say that he was freed and went to live at the court of King Croesus; others that he was killed by the inhabitants of Delphos, who were angered by him and threw him over a cliff. Another tradition has it that he was ugly and deformed. All this is pure guesswork. We can be fairly certain that Aesop's fables are what we call folk tales, handed down among humble people for many generations before they were written in books.

Why have people delighted to hear and repeat these fables for over two thousand years? In the first place, they are clear and simple and easy to remember. Secondly they are wise and sensible, and we see at once that they are true. True to what? They are true to humanity because, although they are mostly about animals, Aesop's animals represent different sides of human nature. The lion stands for kingliness, the ass for obstinate stupidity, the fox for cunning, the sheep for simplicity, the wolf for greed and savagery towards the defenceless. In this way, the various sides of our nature can be seen to be at war with one another; the weak and simple are the victims of the strong and cunning; pride goes before a fall; meddlers often come to harm; patience and skill triumph over life's difficulties. We read Aesop's Fables, not to discover these truths, nor just for the neatness and simplicity of the stories; we read them because, through our pleasure in the stories, we recognize the truths we have always known, but which we delight to meet again in novel form.

The virtues which Aesop praises are not the heroic ones— desperate courage, self-sacrifice, high endeavour; they are the peasant virtues of discretion, prudence, moderation and foresight. They bring hope and consolation to ordinary people, assuring them that the slow can sometimes win the race, that a proud creature may be indebted to a very humble one, that those who lay up store for the winter will be rewarded, and that even the strongest tyrant will fall. That is why Aesop, who—if there ever was such a person—had more than ordinary wisdom, has always had the affection and regard of ordinary people.

It is the qualities of simplicity and directness which I have tried to preserve in this new version of some of the fables. The form in which they are usually presented is too bare and unadorned to reveal all their possibilities. Some of them are scarcely more than brief synopses of what, in the original telling, must have been considerably fuller and more detailed. In particular there is very little direct speech. In putting actual words into the mouths of the animals my aim has been to keep the spirit of the original, while adding nothing except an element of drama and a sense of immediacy. Other attempts have been made to re-tell Aesop, often in verse; I have chosen a simple, direct and colloquial prose as being most likely to appeal to young readers of today. I hope they will share the delight which these indestructible stories have always given me.

James Reeves

FOX AND GOAT

One evening Reynard the Fox left his home and set off for town to see what he could steal for his little ones' supper. In his hurry he fell into a well and couldn't get out. He tried scrambling up the side, but it was no use. Then, just when he was giving up hope and beginning to think he would be drowned, he heard footsteps above. Looking up, he saw the hairy face of Goat peering over the edge of the well.

'Hello,' said Goat. 'Who are you down there?'

'It's only me—Fox,' said Reynard.

'What are you doing down there at this time of night?'

'I was having a drink,' answered Fox.

'Is the water good?' asked Goat. 'It's been a warm day, and I'm feeling a little thirsty myself.'

'Why, the water's delicious!' answered Fox. 'I've never tasted such water in my life. Why don't you come and try it? There's plenty left.'

Without further talk, Goat jumped into the well. This was just what Fox had been hoping for. Without asking Goat whether he minded, he scrambled up on his back, and with the help of Goat's horns he was able to lift himself to safety.

'Thank you, friend Goat,' said Reynard, for he is always polite. 'That was most kind of you. Without your help I might *never* have got out.'

Goat looked up at the top of the well and began to call out piteously.

'Oh dear me! I didn't see how deep it was. How am *I* going to get out?'

'I've no idea,' said Reynard. 'That's *your* affair. Didn't your mother *ever* tell you to look before you leap?'

And with that, Fox turned away and made off towards the town to see what he could steal, leaving poor Goat to get out of the well as best he might.

Look before you leap.

LION AND MOUSE

It was a hot day, and Lion was sleeping under a rock. He was a big lion, very splendid and noble; in fact, as everyone knows, he was King of All Animals. Now it so happened that Mouse had lost her way. Running hither and thither, she stumbled over Lion's very nose and woke him. Instantly Lion put out a paw and held Mouse fast to the ground. Mice, as everyone knows, are very little animals, and this mouse was specially little. But she stuck her head out from under Lion's paw and began to squeak piteously.

 (H 455)

'Oh, Your Majesty,' she squeaked, 'please forgive me. I didn't mean to trip over Your Majesty's nose and wake Your Majesty, truly I didn't. Of course Your Majesty *could* squash me dead with one squash, but would it be worth it for such a noble and dignified animal as a lion to squash such a miserable little creature as a mouse?'

'Stop squeaking!' ordered Lion. 'Tell me why I should be merciful to such an insignificant creature as you.'

'Well,' said Mouse, 'it is a noble act for a King to be merciful. It shows how noble he is. Besides, Your Majesty, perhaps one day even a miserable little creature like me *might* be able to do Your Majesty a good turn. Who knows?'

'Ho, ho, ho!' laughed Lion, King of All Animals, with a great roar that nearly terrified Mouse out of her small wits. 'That's a good one—a mouse help a lion! Well, that's a good joke, upon my whiskers.'

And he twiddled his whiskers to show what fine whiskers they were, and also how amused he was.

'Well, I didn't say it *would* happen,' said Mouse, 'I only said it *might*.'

And *she* twiddled *her* whiskers, just to show that she too had whiskers, even though they were such little whiskers.

'Very well,' said Lion. 'Off you go, and leave me to my sleep. And in future mind where you're going.'

'Oh I will, Your Majesty,' said Mouse. 'Thank you so *very* much for sparing my life.'

But Lion only snored. He was asleep again.

Well, a long time afterwards, Lion was roaming through the jungle, not looking where he was going, because he was King of All Animals and had become just a bit careless, so he fell right into a trap that some hunters had set for him. It was a deep pit covered over with a net hidden by leaves. Into the pit fell Lion with the net all round him, so that he got tangled up in it and couldn't free himself. So he let out a great roar, and the whole jungle shook with his roaring, and every creature in the jungle stopped what he was doing and trembled with fear.

Not far off the little mouse put down a corn-stalk she was nibbling and said to herself: 'Now where have I heard *that* noise before? Why, of course, it's King Lion, and it sounds as if he's in trouble.'

So in less than one minute she had run to the place where Lion was caught in the net, and began to bite through the strings of the net. Soon she had made a hole large enough for Lion to get through, so he was able to escape and wasn't caught by the hunters after all.

I am sorry to say that he didn't thank Mouse quite as graciously as he ought to have done. But Mouse did not mind. She scampered away to look for the corn-stalk she had put down when she heard King Lion's roar.

Kindness is never thrown away—no one is so unimportant that he may not be able to repay a good turn.

TIMOTHY AND THE NETTLE

Timothy was playing in the meadows when he lost his ball. Presently he saw it lying behind a clump of nettles. He put out his hand to take it, and brushing the nettle aside, he was badly stung. He cried with pain and ran in to tell his mother.

'A horrid nettle stung me!' cried Timothy. 'I hardly touched it, and now look what it's done!'

He held out his hand, on which the rash was already showing.

'It was because you hardly touched it,' said his mother, 'that it stung you. Next time you meddle with a nettle, grasp it firmly and it won't hurt you. Go and rub your hand with a dock leaf, and remember what I've told you.'

Whatever you do, do it boldly.

WOLF IN SHEEP'S CLOTHING

Wolf thought of a plan for getting his living more easily.

'If I can manage to live along with those sheep,' he said to himself, 'I can run off with one of them when I get a chance. But if I go like this, the shepherd will notice me and set his dogs on me and drive me off. He might even get a gun and shoot me.'

So he took the skin of a sheep that had died up in the hills, and dressed himself carefully in it, making sure to cover up all his own grey hair. Then he slipped in among the sheep, and wasn't noticed. At night he was shut in the pen, along with the flock.

'When all's quiet,' he thought, with a cunning smile, 'I'll kill one of these fat sheep and have a better meal than I ever had in my life.'

But the shepherd, before going home, remembered

that he had meant to kill a sheep for his own dinner next day. So he took a sharp knife and went back into the pen. But the sheep that he killed in the dark was not a sheep at all—it was Wolf, dressed up in sheep's clothing.

Laziness may be our ruin.

EAGLE AND JACKDAW

Jackdaw sat on the branch of a tree, half-way up a steep hill. Below, in the valley, a shepherd was minding his flock. On a crag at the very top of the hill perched a great eagle, King of All Birds. How noble he looked, with his great wings outstretched, ready to swoop, and his eyes fixed on the ground far below!

Then Jackdaw saw Eagle dive down and seize a lamb from the shepherd's flock. He carried it skywards in his mighty talons, and was lost to sight behind the hill-top.

'What a splendid way of catching your dinner!' thought Jackdaw. 'Why shouldn't I get mine like that?'

So he too swooped down and fell upon an old ram, whose wool was long and fleecy. But the ram was far too big for him, and he got his feet caught up in the creature's long fleeces. He was so hopelessly entangled that he could not escape. The shepherd came up, and had no difficulty in seizing Jackdaw and keeping him prisoner. He disentangled the bird from the ram's wool and clipped his wings so that he could not fly away. Then the shepherd took Jackdaw home as a pet for his little son.

'Thank you, father,' said the boy, 'but what kind of bird is this?'

'It is a jackdaw,' said the shepherd. 'He is only a jackdaw—but he thought himself an eagle!'

Pride goes before a fall.

DONKEY IN LION'S SKIN

One day Donkey found the skin of a lion that had died. He put it on and wore it as if it were his own, covering up his dusty grey hair with the lion's tawny hide.

'What a splendid overcoat!' said Donkey to himself. 'Now I'm just like Lion, King of All Animals.'

So he went prancing about the countryside, frightening all the timid creatures he could find. First he saw Rabbit and galloped up to him, roaring as loudly as he could. Rabbit scuttled away into his burrow.

Then Donkey came upon Goat and frightened him in the same way, till Goat ran up a steep hillside as fast as he could run.

Donkey felt very pleased with himself, and laughed aloud to think how he was playing at being King of the Beasts.

'Why,' he thought, 'I only have to put on Lion's skin to be as fierce and terrible as Lion himself. Here comes Fox! Let's see if I can scare him.'

So as soon as Reynard was near, Donkey crouched as low as he could and tried to look as savage and terrible as Lion.

He growled ferociously, but to Reynard it sounded just like 'Ee-aw! Ee-aw!'

So Reynard only laughed and ran right up to Donkey; he lifted the corner of Lion's skin and saw Donkey's dusty grey hair.

'Good *day*, Your Majesty,' said Reynard slyly. 'I shouldn't be surprised to see a pair of long ears under that mane of yours. Why, what a donkey you are, to think you could frighten me! Whoever heard a lion bray like that?'

And he ran off to tell all the other animals what a donkey Donkey was, and how silly they had been to be scared of him.

If you play a part you are not fitted for, you're sure to give yourself away.

OAK AND REED

A great oak tree stood on a hill, and a slender reed grew at its foot. When the wind blew, the reed swayed and shook, but the oak remained firm.

The tree looked down at the little reed and called to him:

'Why do you tremble so when the wind blows? Why don't you keep still, like me?'

'I'm not as strong as you,' said the reed in his small piping voice. 'I could never stand up in a wind.'

'Then you must be a coward,' said the oak scornfully, 'and a poor sort of plant. You should learn to stand up for yourself. Just take a lesson from me.'

And the oak stood on the hill, taller and stronger than ever.

But soon there came a great storm. A mighty wind blew from off the sea and made a terrible roaring, so that people said they had never heard a gale like this one in all their lives. The oak stood firm and the slender reed bowed before the wind until it touched the ground. All night long the wind blew, and when in the morning it ceased, the reed stood up again, but the oak lay flat on the ground, smashed down by the force of the gale.

The proud will be destroyed, but the humble will outlive their misfortunes.

THE STAG AT THE POOL

Stag went down to a pool to drink. As he lapped the cool water, he noticed his reflection, and said to himself:

'What magnificent antlers I have! How slender and graceful they are, and how delicately curved and branched. But it's a pity about my skinny legs and small feet. They rather spoil my good looks.'

At that moment a hunting horn was heard, and a pack of hounds streamed down the hill towards the pool, followed by two or three huntsmen on horseback.

Instantly Stag stopped drinking and took to his heels. He coursed over the fields until he came to the shelter of a thicket. His legs had carried him beyond the reach of the hounds, but his antlers got caught in the branches of a tree. He only just managed to free himself before the hounds came in sight, and once more he ran for his life. When he had thrown off the pursuit, he stood still, panting and breathless.

'Ah,' said Stag, 'I shouldn't have spoken badly of the legs and feet that nature gave me. They saved my life. As for my beautiful antlers, they were almost my undoing.'

Use is of more importance than ornament.

The Mice were having a war with the Weasels. But Weasels are bigger and fiercer and are more than a match for Mice. So the Mice had a meeting to decide what to do.

'Let's choose leaders,' one of them said. 'We shall never beat the Weasels if each of us fights for himself, and there is no one to give orders. Let us have generals, to give orders and plan the battle.'

Immediately the biggest and strongest Mice pushed themselves forward and said they would be the generals. The others agreed, and once more they went out to battle.

Now the generals, in order to make themselves look bigger and more important than the other Mice, tied

30

horns on their heads. Then everyone would know they were the leaders.

When the Weasels came, the Mice were ready for them. They fought bravely for an hour or more, but many of the Mice were killed, and the generals decided they must retreat. So they gave the order, and all the Mice scuttled back into their holes, which were too small for the Weasels to follow them. But the generals got their tall horns caught, and could not get back into the holes fast enough. So they were set on by the Weasels and quickly destroyed.

After that, no more Mice came forward and offered to be leaders.

There is danger in being a leader.

THE GOD MERCURY

Now, the Romans had many gods. The chief of them all was Jupiter, and his wife was Juno. Their messenger, who used to travel between heaven and earth, was the swift-winged Mercury. One day Mercury thought he would like to know what the people on earth thought about him. Did they think him a great god, he wondered, or did they rate him at little value? Overcome with curiosity, he paid a visit to the earth.

In a certain city there was a sculptor named Lucius, who made clay images of the gods. These he sold to the people to set up in their houses. When Mercury came down to earth, he disguised himself as a traveller and went into Lucius' shop.

'Good day, friend,' he said. 'Have you some figures of the chief gods for sale?'

'I have indeed, sir,' answered the sculptor, stopping his work to wipe his hands on his apron. 'What god are you interested in?'

'How much do you want for this figure of Jupiter?' asked Mercury, picking up a small clay model of the ruler of the gods.

'Well, I could let you have that for a silver piece,' answered Lucius.

'I see,' said Mercury, laughing to himself.

'So that's what the All-High God is worth—one silver piece,' he thought. 'That's not much.'

But he only said:

'And this one of Juno, the goddess of women—how much does that cost?'

'That's a bit more,' answered Lucius. 'I'd have to ask two silver pieces for Juno.'

'Really?' said Mercury. 'Now what about this—how much would you ask for this handsome figure?'

And he picked up a small statue of himself, the god Mercury.

'Oh *that*,' answered the sculptor. This time it was his turn to laugh. 'I can't very well ask much for *him*—let's see. . . . I tell you what. If you give me the price I ask for the other two, I'll throw in Mercury for nothing!'

Mercury was so angry that he stamped out of the shop without another word.

If you try to find out what other people think of you, you may be disappointed.

(H 455)

LEOPARD AND FOX

Leopard was putting the finishing touches to his toilet.
He lay in the sun, admiring the beauty of his sleek,
smooth coat, so elegantly marked. He rose lazily and
strolled over to the pool, the better to gaze at himself
in the clear water.

'R-r-r-really,' he purred, 'I am indeed beautiful. Of
all the animals in the forest, I am certainly the finest.'

'I don't know so much about that,' said Fox, who

was passing at the time and happened to overhear him. Leopard pretended not to hear.

'It's those spots,' went on Reynard more loudly. 'What a pity you can't change them!'

Leopard looked down his nose at Fox in a lordly way.

'And who are you to talk?' he said at last, showing his sharp white teeth and curling his tail scornfully. 'With that scrubby ginger coat of yours and that bedraggled brush, I wonder you dare show yourself in public.'

'I think I heard you say you were the finest creature in the forest,' said Reynard. 'How do you make that out?'

'*You* may not like my spots,' answered Leopard, 'but most creatures admire them greatly. Then I have such sleek, luxuriant fur, such a graceful shape, and such a noble way of moving. But I suppose you think yourself even finer.'

'Indeed I do,' answered Reynard. 'I may not have your spots and your glossy finish. I may not be able to creep about like a snake. But I have brains, my dear chap. I'm the cleverest, craftiest, cunningest animal in the whole creation. Why, everyone envies me my intelligence! As for you, you've no more wit than a hen. *That's* why I'm finer than you!'

And without waiting for an answer he sped off into the woods after a rabbit.

Good looks aren't everything.

35

DOG AND DOG'S REFLECTION

There was once a dog, and a very greedy dog he was. One day he sneaked into a butcher's shop and stole a piece of meat. Such a fine, tender, juicy piece of meat

36

it was! Before the butcher could stop him, he grabbed that meat and scuttled out of the shop as fast as his four legs would take him. Lifting his chopper on high, the butcher ran after him, shouting, 'Stop thief! Stop thief!' But no one could stop Dog. Away he flew, till he was out of town and into the green country. He thought he would take the piece of meat to a quiet spot in the middle of a wood, and there enjoy it without fear of being disturbed.

Now it happened that on his way he had to pass over a low bridge made of a plank laid across a clear stream. When he was on the plank, Dog stopped for a minute to get his breath, for he had been running hard. Looking into the water below, he saw what he thought was another dog just like himself; and in that dog's mouth was a piece of meat—a fine, tender, juicy piece of meat just like his own. In fact, Dog thought it was even better than his own. Of course the dog in the water wasn't real—it was only the reflection of Dog on the bridge. But Dog thought he was real, and wondered why another dog should have a piece of meat as good as his own, or better. So he jumped into the stream and tried to grab the other dog's meat, for he was a greedy dog, as I told you. Well, not only did he get very wet; he also dropped his own meat into the water and never found it again. So in the end Dog got nothing, because he was so greedy.

Hold on to the good things you have: don't lose them by trying to get what isn't really there.

37

WAR-HORSE AND DONKEY

Donkey was toiling along the road bearing a heavy load of stones for repairing the farmyard wall. It was a hot day, and poor Donkey was almost worn out. Presently he heard the thunder of hooves. A splendid war-horse was approaching along the road, his harness jingling and his saddle-cloth flapping gaily as he galloped along.

'Out of my way, Ass!' called the war-horse. 'I am the proud Tarquin, and I am off to the wars.'

Donkey said nothing, but obediently stumbled to the side of the road, just in time to let Tarquin pass.

'Be more careful, you dolt!' shouted Tarquin over his shoulder. 'I nearly trampled you under my hooves.'

Donkey plodded patiently on up the dusty road, while the horse galloped off to the war.

Not long afterwards there was a battle, and Tarquin was wounded. An arrow struck him in the shoulder, and he was so badly hurt that he was no longer fit to be a war-horse. He was put to work on the farm.

One day Donkey saw him struggling into the yard drawing a huge cart. He was panting wearily, and called to Donkey for help.

'Give us a hand with this wagon,' he said. 'I'm not used to this sort of work, and it's killing me.'

'No,' said Donkey. 'You should have thought of that when you nearly trampled on me in the road. I'm having my rest now, and it's no use asking me for help.'

The proud cannot look for help to those they have slighted.

TOWN MOUSE AND COUNTRY MOUSE

Country Mouse lived in a cornfield deep in the country-side. Her life was calm and unexciting. One day a mouse from the town came that way, and Country Mouse invited her to dinner. They sat down in the fields and had a picnic of barley grains.

Town Mouse didn't think much of it.

'Is this how you live all the year round?' she asked, twirling her whiskers. 'Not much to do here, is there?'

'I live well enough,' answered Country Mouse.

'When the weather's fine, I play in the fields. When it's wet, I take shelter in a barn. Nobody bothers me, and I don't have to trouble about looking smart or entertaining fine visitors.'

'But is this all you have to eat?' asked Town Mouse in a very haughty voice.

'It's plain,' said Country Mouse, 'but it's wholesome; and there's plenty of it. I never go short of a meal, and I never have a day's illness. You should come and stay with me some time.'

'I should die of boredom,' said Town Mouse, hiding a yawn behind her well-groomed paw. 'But you'd better visit me. Then you'll see what life can be like.'

So next day Country Mouse went to dinner with Town Mouse.

'What a fine place you have, to be sure!' she said, admiring the great house and the pretty garden, full of flowers and vegetables of all sorts.

Town Mouse lived in a larder, which was always stored with meats and cheeses of every description.

'Yes, indeed,' said Town Mouse. 'This is something like life! Why, there's never a dull moment! Come on, let's have dinner. Now, what will you take? I can give you a little roast chicken—or will you begin with cheese and biscuits? I have a particularly fine gorgonzola this week.'

'Well, that's very kind of you,' said Country Mouse. 'Now which shall it be? I rather think——'

But just at that moment the door of the larder was pushed open, and a pair of heavy boots walked in.

'Look out,' said Town Mouse. 'We'd better hide behind this bread bin for a minute or two.'

The two mice went into hiding. Country Mouse could see that Town Mouse was trembling with fear.

'As you say,' she said when the boots had gone, 'never a dull moment. Well, suppose I try a little cheese?'

No sooner had she got her teeth into the gorgonzola than the boots came back. Nasty, big, ugly things they were too! Once more the mice scuttled behind the bread bin till the intruder had gone. This time the door was left open, so the poor mice stayed behind the bin, nibbling their dinner and scarcely daring to speak. All at once there was a sound of paws, and a grey cat snuffed her way into the larder. Town Mouse dropped what she was eating and took flight down a hole in the floor. Country Mouse followed her, but she didn't wait any longer. Instead, she told Town Mouse that this sort of life would be the death of her, and ran off back to the country as fast as she could go.

She sat down in her own cornfield and began eating a barley grain.

'This is the life for me,' she said to herself. 'Let Town Mouse keep her fine house and her splendid food. It would never suit me. What's the good of all the meat and cheese in the world if you can never sit down and enjoy it in peace?'

A plain life and a safe one is better than fine fare without security.

MONKEY AND FISHERMEN

Monkey sat in a palm tree overlooking the river.
Presently two fishermen came along. They carried
a net between them, which they stretched from
bank to bank, so that it hung down in the water. In
this way they would catch the fish that swam up or
down the stream. Then the two men went away
to eat their dinner and wait.

'That's a good idea,' thought Monkey, and as
soon as the fishermen were out of sight, he
jumped down from the tree. He ran to a spot
where he knew there was an old fishing net; and
this he dragged down to the water and tried to do
the same as he had seen the men do. But he had
never tried fishing before, and very soon he got so
tangled up in the net that he nearly drowned. He
choked and spluttered in the water, and it was
only with the greatest difficulty that he managed
to tear himself free and get safely to shore.

'That's the last time I go fishing,' he said to himself. 'In future I'd better stick to coconuts.'

Don't meddle with what you don't understand.

ANT AND GRASSHOPPER

All summer the ant had been working hard, gathering a store of corn for the winter. Grain by grain she had taken it from the fields and stowed it away in a hole in the bank, under a hawthorn bush.

One bright, frosty day in winter Grasshopper saw her. She was dragging out a grain of corn to dry it in the sun. The wind was keen, and poor Grasshopper was cold.

'Good morning, Ant,' said he. 'What a terrible winter it is! I'm half dead with hunger. Please give me just one of your corn grains to eat. I can find nothing, although I've hopped all over the farmyard. There isn't a seed to be found. Spare me a grain, I beg.'

'Why haven't you saved anything up?' asked Ant. '*I* worked hard all through the summer, storing food for the winter. Very glad I am too, for as you say, it's bitterly cold.'

'I wasn't idle last summer, either,' said Grasshopper.

'And what did you do, pray?'

'Why, I spent the time singing,' answered Grasshopper. 'Every day from dawn till sunset I jumped about or sat in the sun, chirruping to my heart's content.'

''Oh you did, did you?' replied Ant. 'Well, since you've sung all summer to keep yourself cheerful, you

may dance all winter to keep yourself warm. Not a
grain will I give you!'

And she scuttled off into her hole in the bank, while
Grasshopper was left cold and hungry.

In good times prepare for when the bad times come.

LION AND FOX

One day King Lion sent to Fox to come and speak with him. Reynard obeyed. Bowing deeply before the king, he said:

'What can I do for Your Majesty?'

Lion looked down his royal nose at the sly little creature before him.

'Fox,' he said graciously, 'you are a crafty and resourceful animal.'

Reynard bowed his head, and wondered what was coming next.

'My eyesight is not what it was,' Lion went on. 'When I go hunting, I don't see my prey as easily as I used to. I am a fierce and deadly hunter, but I have need of a servant to find my prey and point him out to me. Will you do this? I will see that you have a share in whatever I kill. I, of course, will have the lion's share, but you shall not go hungry.'

Reynard gladly accepted this honourable position, and became King Lion's servant.

For a time all went well. Fox would lead Lion through the thickets and among the rocks, and whenever his sharp little eyes caught sight of a goat or a deer, he would signal noiselessly to his master. Lion would instantly bound towards the helpless creature and kill it. And he always gave Reynard a share.

But one day Reynard said to himself:

46

'This is all very fine. Hunting is now an easy matter for the king, since he has my sharp eyes and keen nose to depend on. He may be brawny, but I am the brains of the partnership. Why should he have all the fun of the kill? Besides, everyone says what a mighty hunter he is. Nobody thinks of me.'

So he said to Lion:

'Your Majesty, now that I have seen you hunt, I think I know something about it. I would like to do the killing myself. Will you allow me to have a try?'

'By all means, my dear fellow,' said Lion. 'Just you go ahead.'

Fox, very pleased with himself, soon spied out a herd of deer, and without waiting for Lion to follow him, he sped towards them. At that instant a huntsman on a swift horse rode up in pursuit of the herd. Catching sight of Fox, he reined in his horse and lifted his gun to his shoulder. A bullet whistled past Reynard's ear, and at the sound of the gun he nearly died of fright. He gave up chasing the herd and returned to King Lion, looking very sorry for himself. After that, he left the killing to his master and contented himself with pointing out the prey.

Do the work you are suited for, and don't attempt what is beyond you.

WOLF AND CRANE

Once Wolf got a bone stuck in his throat. He had been greedy and eaten his meat too fast. The bone was sharp and gave him great pain. In vain he coughed and choked. The bone would not come out. He howled and screeched aloud.

48

'Help me, some creature!' he cried, as best he could. 'Won't someone pull this bone out of my throat? Come along, Fox, you try.'

But the fox refused. So did all the other animals. They hated Wolf, and no one was willing to help him.

'If someone doesn't help me, I shall die,' moaned Wolf. 'If anyone gets this bone out, I'll give him a handsome reward.'

Now the crane, a tall bird with a long bill, happened to be passing and overheard the wolf's lament. He took pity on him and offered to help. Besides, the idea of a reward tempted him.

'I can do him a good turn, poor fellow,' he thought, 'and get something for myself into the bargain.'

So Crane put his long bill down into Wolf's throat, seized the bone, and gave it a sharp tug. Wolf howled with pain, but the bone came out.

'There,' said Crane, 'that's got it. I hope you're feeling better. Now what about my reward?'

'What reward?' snarled Wolf, showing his yellow teeth. 'Why, you ungrateful bird! You've just put your head down the throat of a wolf without getting it bitten off. No other creature has done that! And that's your reward, you lucky bird! Fly away, before I gobble you up.'

Crane didn't stop to argue, but did as he was told.

Those who help a rogue in hope of gain mustn't grumble if their trouble goes unrewarded.

BIRDCATCHER AND PARTRIDGE

Peter was a birdcatcher. He used to go out with his nets and lay them cunningly among the bushes, so that birds in search of food would get caught in them. Then he would kill them and sell them in the market. One day he caught a fat partridge. The bird cried out piteously and spoke to Peter.

'Oh Mr. Birdcatcher, I beg you to let me go. I never did you any harm. Oh, spare my life, I beg you!'

'I don't know so much about that,' said Peter. 'Why should I let you go, eh?'

'If you will spare my life,' answered the partridge, 'I might be useful to you. I can sit beside your net and attract other birds into it. As you know, birds of a feather flock together; and many a young partridge will I lead into your snare.'

'Why, you miserable traitor!' cried Peter scornfully. 'I might have let you go, but now I shall do no such thing. No creature deserves to live who is cowardly enough to save his own skin by betraying his friends.'

Only a coward betrays his fellows.

THE MILLER, THE BOY, AND THE DONKEY

Old John the Miller was a good-natured man, and always tried to please everyone.

'We don't need that donkey any more,' said his wife. 'You can get a good price for him now, John, if you take him into town next market day.'

So Old John set off with his young son Jack, and led the donkey along the road to the town.

Presently a party of girls passed them, and when they saw the miller and his donkey, they laughed.

'Fancy walking to town on a hot day like this,' one of them said, 'when you've got a donkey to carry you!'

Old John hadn't thought of this.

'Why of course,' he said. 'Up you get, my boy, and let him save you a walk.'

He helped Jack on to the donkey's back, and off they went once more.

Soon they passed a company of old men sitting outside an inn.

'Well, I declare!' said one old man. 'Do you see that? Look at that young lad riding the donkey, while the old man has to walk alongside!'

'Ay,' said another, 'just what I was saying. Young folks are all selfish nowadays, and never think of their elders. Hi, young 'un, let the old man have a turn on the Donkey!'

'Perhaps they're right,' said the miller. 'Would you

mind getting down now, Jack, and letting your old father have a ride?'

So Jack and his father changed places, and jogged on towards the town. Very soon they came up with a party of women, and one of them said:

'Now, isn't that too bad! Just look at the selfish old man, riding on the donkey, while the little lad runs along behind! The poor little chap can hardly keep up with him. It's downright cruel, that it is, on a day like this.'

'Well, perhaps you'd better come up behind me,' said Old John to his son. 'I think there's room for both.'

So with both of them astride the donkey, they reached the outskirts of the town. Here they were met by a townsman, out for a walk with his dog. He looked at them and said:

'How can you have the heart to overload that poor beast on a day like this? You're just as well able to carry that old donkey between you, you two, as he is to carry you!'

'Just as you say,' said Old John, anxious to please the townsman. And indeed, the donkey was somewhat the worse for wear. So he and Jack got down from his back and tied his four legs together. They took a strong pole, thrust it between the donkey's legs, and hoisted him on to their shoulders. Then with the donkey swinging upside down between them, the miller and his son made their way into the town.

Well, they looked so ridiculous that all the people

came out to see them. How they laughed and cheered to see such a strange sight! Just as they reached a bridge over the river that runs beside the town, the donkey was alarmed by the cheering and shouting, as well as by his extreme discomfort. So he kicked with all his might and broke loose from the pole. But he couldn't stop himself from plunging over the side of the bridge, and falling with a great splash into the water.

'That's what comes of trying to suit everyone,' said the old man in disgust. 'Come on, my boy, let's be getting home.'

Old John the Miller had lost his donkey, and there was nothing for it but to turn round and go back the way he had come.

It's no use trying to please everyone.

WIDOW MARTIN AND HER HEN

Old Jenny Martin was a widow who lived by herself. She had one fine hen which laid her an egg a day, a beautiful fresh egg with a smooth brown shell. Not content with this, she said to herself:

'Every day I give that hen two handfuls of barley, and she lays me one egg. Now if I was to give her *four* handfuls, perhaps she'd lay me *two* eggs.'

So she went to the bin and took out four handfuls of barley, and the hen pecked it all up in no time.

Next morning the widow went hopefully to the hen-house, but there was still only one egg. The day after, it was the same. Widow Martin gave the hen four handfuls, but she only got one egg in exchange. Worse than that, the extra food soon made the hen so fat and lazy that she stopped laying altogether. So poor Widow Martin had no eggs at all.

Figures don't always work out as we want them to.

BIRDS, BEASTS, AND BAT

Long, long ago there was a war between the birds and the beasts. Eagle and Hawk swooped down and carried off little creatures like Mole and Rabbit; and to get their revenge, Serpent and Cat stole the birds' eggs from their nests and killed the birds whenever they could catch them. Every creature in the world took sides—except one, Bat.

'I will see which is strongest,' said Bat to himself, 'and take whichever side looks like winning.'

With his great leathery wings he could easily pass for a bird, and with his ears and claws he could equally well be taken for a beast.

When the beasts were doing well, and looked like killing all the birds, Bat said he was a beast and fought against the birds. But when the birds were doing well, he flew round like a bird and killed little mice in the fields and hedges. It was a fierce war and went on for many months.

At last both beasts and birds grew tired of fighting and made peace. Both sides promised never to start another war, though I am sorry to say they have not always kept their word. But because of the way he had behaved during the fighting, neither side would have Bat.

'You fought for the beasts!' cried the eagle, King of Birds. 'You may go and be a beast.'

'You were on the side of the birds,' said Lion, King
of All Animals, 'so of course you must be a bird!'

So from that day to this, Bat has never really been
sure whether he is beast or bird, and has skulked about
by night and made his home in the roofs of barns. He
flies like a bird, but does not sit in the trees by day and
sing. So nobody knows exactly what kind of creature
he is.

No one likes a turncoat.

FOX AND GRAPES

Reynard was hungry. For two whole days he had had nothing to eat. Not a rabbit had he caught in the fields; not a hen had he stolen from the farm. He began to think he would die of starvation. That night, when everyone was in bed, and the moon was peeping over

the hill, he crept into a rich man's garden to have a look round. He sniffed inquisitively. All at once he noticed a most delicious smell. It was the smell of sweet, juicy grapes. Reynard looked up. There they were, bunches and bunches of the big purple fruit, all ripe and ready to be picked. He licked his lips greedily and stretched himself upwards. But even when he stood on his hind legs so that he nearly fell over backwards, they were still out of reach. So he crouched down almost to the ground and gave a mighty leap in the air. He couldn't even reach the lowest bunch. Reynard looked round for another way to get at them. But it was useless. The vine grew high against the wall of the rich man's house, and all the fruit was growing on the upper branches. Once more he took a few steps backwards and sprang at the grapes. Again and again he jumped, but not a single grape could he pull down. So when he was too tired to jump any more, he turned away and slunk out of the garden.

'Let the grapes rot!' he said angrily. 'They're not worth bothering about. Anyone can see they're sour!'

People sometimes speak ill of what they can't get.

'WOLF! WOLF!'

Paul was a shepherd boy who lived in a village not far from a great forest. Every day he went out to the fields to mind his master's sheep. Now there were wolves in that forest, and Paul thought he would play a joke on the people of his village. One day he shouted out at the top of his voice, in a tone of great alarm:

'Wolf! Wolf! Come quickly—the wolf is after my sheep!'

Some of the villagers came rushing out with sticks and stones to drive away the enemy. But when they reached Paul, he was laughing at them.

'How funny you all look,' he said, 'charging through the fields with your sticks and stones to frighten away a wolf that isn't here! Oh dear, I shall never stop laughing.'

Angrily the villagers went back home. They didn't think Paul's joke was at all funny.

A week or so later he played the same trick. The villagers thought he must really be in trouble this time. Once more they ran to his help, and once more they found the sheep safe and sound, with not a wolf in sight.

'The boy's a liar,' one of the villagers said. 'He won't get *me* out again with his lying tales!'

Then a few days later a wolf *did* come out of the forest, and ran straight towards one of Paul's sheep.

'Wolf! Wolf!' cried Paul, terrified. 'Help me, good neighbours, I pray. Help, help!'

But this time the villagers who heard him said to each other:

'There's that wicked boy up to his tricks again! But he won't make a fool of us this time.'

And they took no notice and went on with their work.

With no one to help him, Paul could not drive away the wolf, which pounced upon the sheep and ran off with it into the forest. So Paul's thoughtless joke had cost his master one of his flock.

Liars are not believed even when they tell the truth.

VENUS AND THE CAT

Once upon a time there was a cat who fell in love with a handsome young man. She prayed and prayed to Venus, the Goddess of Love, to give her the young man for a husband. So Venus, taking pity on the cat, changed her into a beautiful young lady. The man saw her and instantly fell in love. So the two were married, and the man took home the young lady as his bride.

But had she really changed, or was she still a cat underneath? Venus wanted to find out.

One day the goddess sent a little mouse into the lady's house, where she was sitting with her husband. At first the young lady did not notice the mouse, but suddenly she saw it. She made a quick movement and sprang upon it, and almost before the young man had seen the mouse, it was dead.

'So,' said Venus to herself, 'she may *look* like a young lady, but she behaves like a cat.'

And the goddess was so angry that she changed the young lady back into a cat, and the young man never saw her again.

We cannot change our true nature.

THE OLD LADY AND HER MAIDS

There was once an old lady who kept two maids called Sally and Sue. She worked them very hard, for she was a mean old lady and liked to get all she could for her money. But Sally and Sue didn't mind hard work: what they minded was having to get up the moment the cock crew. For that is what the old lady made them do.

Every morning, whether it was at five o'clock or four, as soon as the cock crew in the yard, the old lady called to Sally and Sue to bestir themselves and begin the day's work.

'This won't do at all,' said Sally. 'I hate that old cock, I do.'

'So do I,' said Sue. 'If only he'd forget to crow, we might get a bit of sleep for once.'

'I tell you what,' said Sally, 'let's get rid of him. Then he can't crow any more.'

So they went to the yard when the old lady was out visiting one day, and wrung the cock's neck, so that he would never more wake them up in the morning.

But now the old lady missed the sound of 'Cock-a-doodle-do' in the morning, and she was so worried for fear the maids would oversleep, that she took to calling them herself. She wasn't content with four or five o'clock—she sometimes woke at midnight and made the girls get up earlier than ever. So Sally and Sue did themselves no good by killing the cock.

It doesn't pay to be too clever.

THE DONKEY'S SHADOW

A young man had to make a journey from one city to another, so he hired a donkey and a driver to take him.

The young man sat on the donkey, and the driver walked beside him, urging the animal forward whenever he didn't go fast enough.

But the day was hot, and towards noon the heat grew unbearable. They were in the middle of a stony desert without a tree or bush in sight. The young man said he could go no farther, so he got off the donkey and sat down in its shadow. But the driver had something to say about that.

'That's *my* place,' he said. 'Move over and let me sit there!'

'Certainly not,' said the young man. 'I hired this donkey for the whole journey, didn't I?'

'You hired the donkey, to be sure,' agreed the driver. 'But you didn't hire his shadow. That belongs to me!'

So the driver and the young man fell to arguing and quarrelling, and in the midst of their quarrel the donkey grew tired of standing still, took to his heels and made off as fast as he could go.

So both the young man and the driver were left in the middle of the desert with nothing but their own feet to get them out of it.

It doesn't always pay to argue.

FOX AND CROW

Crow sat on the branch of a tree with a piece of cheese
in his beak. He had just stolen it from a farm kitchen,
where he had seen it through the open window.
Reynard the Fox looked up and saw Crow on the
branch, and he thought how much *he* would enjoy that
fine fresh piece of cheese.

'Good day, Crow,' said Reynard. But Crow said
nothing. He had the cheese in his beak.

'You know,' Reynard went on, 'I've never really noticed what a beautiful bird you are.'

Crow bent down slightly in order to hear better.

'The smoothness and blackness of your coat is so handsome, so dignified. Your feathers are much lovelier—to my mind—than Peacock's. His are *so* gaudy, don't you think?'

Still Crow said nothing. But he was most interested.

'Then your neck,' Reynard continued, 'why, it is as proud and noble as Eagle's, and everyone knows that he is King of Birds. As for your eye—not even Hawk has a brighter and more resplendent eye! Yes indeed, but for *one* thing, I would say you are worthy to be King of all the birds.'

Crow was preening himself and pluming himself with pride. He had never been so flattered in all his life.

'Yes,' sighed Fox, 'what a pity it is that with all your beauty you should have no voice! If only you knew how to sing.'

This was too much for poor Crow. Perhaps he hadn't a voice like Nightingale's, but at least he could 'caw' in a way which some listeners might not think too bad. He would show Reynard! So taking a deep breath and closing his eyes, he opened his beak and gave out a loud 'Caw, caw!'

Of course the cheese instantly fell out of his mouth, and Reynard caught it and gobbled it up.

Never listen to flattery.

HARE AND TORTOISE

When Tortoise was very little, his mother said to him, 'You will never be able to go very fast. We Tortoises are a slow-moving family, but we get there in the end.

Don't try to run. Remember, "steady and slow" does it.' Tortoise remembered these words.

One day when he was grown up, he was walking quietly round in a field minding his own business; and Hare thought he would have some fun, so he ran round Tortoise in quick circles, just to annoy him. Hare was proud of himself because everyone knew he was one of the swiftest of animals. But Tortoise took no notice, so Hare stopped in front of him and laughed.

'Can't you move faster than *that*?' said Hare. 'You'll *never* get anywhere at that rate! You should take a few lessons from *me*.

Tortoise lifted his head slowly and said:

'I don't want to get anywhere, thank you. I've no need to go dashing about all over the place. You see, my thick shell protects me from my enemies.'

'But how *dull* life must be for you!' Hare went on. 'Why, it takes you half an hour to cross one field, while I can be away out of sight in half a minute. Besides, you really do look silly, you know! You ought to be ashamed of yourself.'

Well, at this Tortoise was rather annoyed. Hare was really very provoking.

'Look here,' said Tortoise, 'if you want a race, I'll give you one; and I don't need any start either.'

Hare laughed till the tears ran down his furry face, and his sides shook so much that he rolled over backwards. Tortoise just waited till Hare had finished, then he said:

'Well, what about it? I'm not joking.'

Several other animals had gathered round, and they all said: 'Go on, Hare. It's a challenge. You'll have to race him.'

'Certainly,' said Hare, 'if you want to make a fool of yourself. Where shall we race to?'

Tortoise shaded his eyes with one foot and said:

'See that old windmill on the top of the hill yonder? We'll race to that. We can start from this tree-stump here. Come on, and may the best animal win!'

So as soon as they were both standing beside the tree-stump, Chanticleer the Cock shouted 'Ready—steady—go!' and Tortoise began to crawl towards the far-off windmill. The other animals had hurried on ahead so as to see the finish.

Hare stood beside the tree-stump watching Tortoise waddle away across the field. The day was hot, and just beside the tree-stump was a pleasant, shady place, so he sat down and waited. He guessed it would take him about two and a half minutes to reach the windmill, even without trying very hard, so there was no hurry—no hurry at all. Presently he began to drop off to sleep. Two or three minutes passed, and Hare opened one eye lazily. Tortoise had scarcely crossed the first field. 'Steady and slow,' he said to himself under his breath. 'Steady and slow. That's what mother said.' And he kept on towards the far-off windmill.

'At that rate,' said Hare to himself sleepily, 'it'll take him just about two hours to get there—if he doesn't drop dead on the way.'

He closed his eye again and fell into a deep sleep.

After a while Tortoise had crossed the first field, and was making his way slowly over the second.

'Steady and slow does it,' he muttered to himself.

The sun began to go down, and at last Hare woke up, feeling chilly.

71

'Where am I?' he thought, 'What's happened? Oh yes, I remember.'

He got to his feet and looked towards the windmill. But where was Tortoise? He was nowhere to be seen. Hare jumped on to the tree-stump and strained his eyes to gaze into the distance. There, half-way across the very last field before the windmill, was a tiny black dot. Tortoise!

'This won't do,' said Hare. 'I must have overslept. I'd better be moving.'

So he sprang from the stump and darted across the first field, then the second, then the third. It was really much farther than he had thought.

At the windmill the other animals were waiting to see the finish. At last Tortoise arrived, rather out of breath and wobbling a little on his legs.

'Come on, Tortoise!' they shouted.

Then Hare appeared at the far side of the last field, streaking along like the wind. How he ran! Not even Stag, when he was being hunted, could go faster. Even Swallow could scarcely fly faster through the blue sky.

'Steady and slow,' said Tortoise to himself, but no one could hear him, for he had very, very little breath left to talk with.

'Come on, Tortoise!' cried some animals, and a few cried, 'Come on, Hare! He's beating you!'

Hare put on extra speed and ran faster than he had ever run before. But it was no good. He had given Tortoise too much start, and he was still twenty yards behind when Tortoise crawled over the last foot of ground and tumbled up against the windmill. He had won the race!

All the animals cheered, and after that Hare never laughed at Tortoise again.

Slow and steady wins the race.

LION, GOAT, AND VULTURE

It was a hot day. Lion and Goat were both thirsty, but the pool was small. Goat bent down his head to drink, when Lion came up beside him and growled fiercely. 'I shall drink first,' he said. 'I am King of All the Animals, and it is my right. Get out of my way!'

'No,' said Goat, '*I* shall drink first. I found the water. You can wait till I've finished.'

'You'll drink it all up,' said Lion. 'There's not very much left, and I am nearly dead with thirst.'

'And I haven't had a drop all day,' answered Goat.

So they quarrelled. Lion chased Goat to the top of a great rock, and, hot as he was, Goat bounded out of the way. Neither of them was able to drink in peace.

Suddenly Lion stopped chasing Goat and looked up into the hot blue sky. Goat looked too. There, circling slowly above them, was Vulture. All the animals knew and feared him. He is the Bird of Death, who waits to pounce on the bodies of dead animals and eat their flesh. Lion and Goat knew, both at once, that if they did not stop fighting, they would die of thirst, and Vulture would pick their bodies to the bone.

'If we go on quarrelling,' said Lion, 'we shall both die of thirst, and that will be the end of us. Go to the water and drink, but don't take it all!'

Goat did as he was told, and the two animals quenched their thirst instead of fighting.

When a common danger threatens, it is best to stop quarrelling.

75

BOAR AND FOX

Fox was walking in the woods one day when he heard a rasping sound.

'I wonder what that can be,' he said to himself, and went on cautiously.

Presently he came to a clearing, and there, sharpening his tusks on a tree trunk, stood a wild boar. How keen and white his two pointed tusks looked! Reynard stood and watched.

'Now tell me why you're doing that,' he said at length.

'I have to keep my tusks sharp,' said Boar, pausing in his work. 'They're my only weapons, you know. I'm not a swift runner like you, and I haven't got claws like a tiger. So when I fight, I have to use my teeth.'

'But there isn't a huntsman or a hound in sight,' answered Reynard. 'You've nothing to fear.'

'Perhaps not,' was the reply, 'but when the hunters and the dogs *do* come after me, it'll be too late to sharpen my weapons *then*.'

And Wild Boar took no further notice of Fox, but went on pointing his tusks against the tree.

When the enemy is upon you, it is too late to make ready your weapons.

TOM IN THE RIVER

Tom splashed lazily about in the river. The day was warm. There was no wind, and the sun shone down out of a clear blue sky. He was only a little boy and had not yet learnt to swim properly, so of course he shouldn't have gone into the middle of the water, out of his depth. Suddenly he discovered that he couldn't touch the bottom.

Tom tried to struggle to safety; then he saw a stranger coming towards him.

'Help!' he shouted as loudly as he could. 'Help me, or I shall drown!'

The stranger came slowly up to the bank. He was a tall, solemn man in black clothes.

'Dear, dear!' said the stranger. 'What a foolish boy you are! Now how did you get into such difficulties? Surely you knew that the water was too deep for you. Did your dear father and mother never tell you not to go into deep water until you could swim? Now if you were a strong swimmer like *me*——'

And so he went on preaching at Tom until the poor boy was almost drowned. But Tom managed to find a place where the water was not so deep, and was able to scramble to the bank.

'You might have helped me,' he said, when he had got his breath again, 'instead of giving me a lecture. You could have done that after I was safe on shore!'

A helping hand is better than a sermon.

MICE AND CAT

The mice all met together one day, very secretly in a safe, dry cellar, to talk about Cat. They had been having a dreadful time lately. Cat was always on the prowl. It seemed that mistress gave him no food and little milk, so that he hunted the mice day and night. They never had a moment's peace. Only last night he had killed no fewer than five of them. So you can understand that the meeting of mice was a very angry one; if the cellar had not been such a safe cellar, Cat would certainly have heard their angry squeakings.

'I suggest,' said one mouse, 'that we all live down here. Cat doesn't seem to know about this place.'

'That's all very well,' said another, 'but we've got to go out sometimes and look for food.'

'Suppose we move to a different house?' said a third mouse.

'Yes, but which?' someone objected. 'There are plenty of mice in most of the houses round here, and they won't welcome us!'

'Besides, there's good eating here.'

'Yes, we're used to it. This is our home! Why should we move? Let Cat move.'

'That's right,' said several mice. 'Let's get rid of Cat.'

'Poison his milk!' said one mouse.

'Set fire to his tail!' suggested another.

'Attack him all together, and bite him to pieces!'

The meeting was getting nowhere, and the mice had become very disorderly, as well as noisy. Then the smallest mouse of all hopped on to an old flower-pot so that he could be seen, and piped up in a high nervous voice:

'May I speak, p-please? I think I've g-got an idea.'

One mouse laughed, but another said, 'Go on, young 'un!' and others said, "Let him speak' and 'Quiet, everyone!' and 'Out with it, then!'

The very smallest mouse cleared his throat and began.

'The trouble is,' he said, 'we never know when Cat's coming. He's so quiet and stealthy, he just creeps up on us before we catch sight or smell of him.'

'That's right. But how can we help it?'

'Quiet, you, and let the little 'un go on!'

'Well,' went on the smallest mouse, 'I know where there's an old rusty bell. It's not very big, but it makes a good clear ring when you shake it. I know 'cos me and my sister plays with it sometimes. Well, I thought that if we were to tie that bell round Cat's neck so that he couldn't get it off, we'd always know when he was coming, and we could get out of the way in time.'

This seemed to be a wonderful idea. Why had no one thought of it before? Of course! Tie a bell to Cat, and he would never trouble them any more. There was loud cheering and squeaking for joy, and everyone shouted 'Hooray! That's the best idea so far. Let's have a vote on it!' And several mice shook the smallest mouse by the paw and slapped him on the back till he was quite dazed and fell off the flower-pot.

'Very well,' shouted the most important mouse, rapping on the floor with a nutshell, 'let's take a vote. Paws up for tying a bell round Cat's neck!'

'Just *one* moment,' said the very oldest mouse, getting shakily to his feet and speaking to the meeting for the first time. So far he had just sat quietly in a corner. He was very old and very grey, and all the mice knew he was extremely wise, except when he was asleep, as he nearly always was.

'I think,' said he, 'this is an excellent plan. If we could attach this bell to our enemy, we should indeed, as our young friend has pointed out, be warned of his approach and be able to get away in time. But before we vote on this proposal, there is just *one* question I should like to ask—and I think we ought to consider it most seriously.'

'Out with it!' said a mouse. 'Get it off your chest, Gaffer!'

The oldest mouse took no notice of the interruption, for being rather deaf, he had scarcely heard it.

'Which of you,' he went on, speaking slowly and gravely—'which of you is going to tie this bell round Cat's neck?'

Nobody said a word. There was not a sound. You could have heard a corn-seed drop.

'Dash my whiskers!' thought the smallest mouse to himself. 'I *never* thought of that.'

As for the oldest mouse of all, he sat down again in his corner, and fell asleep immediately.

And to this very day, mice have never known how to get the better of Cat.

Before deciding on a plan, find out if it can be carried out.

ANT AND DOVE

Ant was thirsty, and going to a pool to drink, she fell in and was almost drowned. Now it happened that a dove was sitting on the branch of a tree overhanging the water. With her sharp eyes she saw the danger that Ant was in, and dropped a leaf, which alighted on the pool. It fell just in front of Ant, who quickly climbed on to it and floated to safety on the bank.

At that very moment a birdcatcher came along with his net, and was just spreading it out to catch the dove. Ant saw what he was trying to do, and noticing that the birdcatcher went barefoot, he bit him in the heel. It was not a very savage bite, but it was the worst that Ant could do; and it was enough to make the bird-catcher jump in the air with surprise. He lost hold of his net, so Dove was just able to escape with her life.

One good turn deserves another.

THE BALD KNIGHT

There was once a Knight who, as he grew old, lost all his hair. His head became as bald as a duck's egg. He didn't want everyone to see how bald he was, so he had a wig made—a fine white wig with long curling tresses.

The very first day he put it on, he went hunting with a company of lords and ladies. Away they went over the green fields and through the forest, with the hounds racing on ahead, and a gay blowing of horns. The Knight was proud of his new wig, as he cantered along on his black horse.

'How handsome they must all think me!' he said to himself.

Presently the hounds lost the scent, and most of the company gathered together under a grove of oak trees till they could pick it up once more. The Knight rode up to join them. Then a dreadful thing happened. He passed under a tree, and as he did so, his wig was caught on a branch and pulled off his head in full view

of everyone. How they laughed, and how foolish the poor Knight looked, after thinking himself so handsome! There he sat on his black horse, while the fine curly wig hung above his head on the oak branch.

The Knight could not help seeing the fun, so he laughed as merrily as anyone else.

'Why,' he said, almost rolling off his horse with amusement, 'how could I expect a wig to stay on my head, when my own hair wouldn't!'

When others laugh at us, it is best to laugh with them.

WIND AND SUN

Wind and Sun had an argument one day, about which was the stronger.

'*I* am the stronger,' boasted Wind, puffing out his cheeks and blowing so hard that every leaf on the trees shook. 'You sit up there, Sun, and do nothing but shine—that is, when I don't blow the clouds across the sky. When *that* happens, you can't even be seen! Of course I'm the stronger.'

'Don't be too sure,' answered Sun calmly, filling the air with his warm radiance. 'I'll tell you what. We'll have a contest, shall we?'

'Certainly,' said Wind. 'Then everyone will know, once for all, who is the stronger. What shall the contest be?'

'See that fellow over there?' said Sun, gazing across the countryside towards a winding, white road. Along it walked a traveller with a cloak about his shoulders.

'I see him,' said Wind.

'Well then, let's see which of us can get his cloak off first.'

'With all my heart!' agreed Wind. 'That's easy. I'll have his cloak off his back in no time.'

So saying, he began to blow. Phoo—oo—oo! The traveller on the road took no notice. But Wind had scarcely begun. He blew harder, and then harder still, till the water of the lakes turned to great waves, and the trees were bent almost double, and the birds in the air were dashed hither and thither with the force of the gale. But the traveller, instead of taking his cloak off, only held it closer round him; and the harder Wind blew, the tighter he clutched it. It was no good. Even when Wind roared like a thousand demons, and blew so as to snap the branches from the stoutest oaks, he could not get the traveller's cloak off his back. At last Wind was tired out and could blow no more. It was Sun's turn. By now the sky was all covered over with dark storm-clouds, but as soon as Wind stopped blowing they gently drifted apart, and Sun shone warmly down over the green fields. Warmer and warmer grew the air under his pleasant beams, and soon the traveller unbuttoned his cloak and let it hang loosely about him. Thanks to Sun's kindly heat he was soon glad to take it off altogether and carry it over his arm.

'There!' said Sun. 'Which of us got it off—tell me that.'

Wind only growled and said nothing. But he knew he was beaten. Sun was the stronger after all.

Gentleness achieves more than violence.

DONKEY CARRYING SALT

There was once a shopkeeper who heard that salt could be bought very cheaply down by the sea. So he took a great basket, tied it to his donkey, and set out for the shore. He filled the basket to the very top with good white salt. Then he tied the lid on securely and started for home, leading Donkey behind him with a rope round his neck. Donkey didn't like the heavy load, but he struggled along with it, until they came to a river which they had to cross. Donkey slipped on

a rock in the middle of the river, and fell over. When he got to his feet again, the water had washed away most of the salt, so of course he found the load much lighter.

'What a bit of luck!' said Donkey to himself. 'I should never have thought of that.'

Next day the shopkeeper went to the sea to get more salt. Once again he filled up the basket and set off, leading Donkey along by the rope. When they came to the river, Donkey remembered what had happened the day before, and slipped over on purpose. Once more they reached home without any salt.

But the shopkeeper had seen what happened.

'We'll put an end to tricks like that!' he said to himself.

Next time, when he got to the sea, he loaded up the basket, not with salt but with sponges. Donkey didn't know the difference, and once again he managed to tumble into the water on purpose, in order to get rid of his load.

But the sponges weren't washed away. They had been dry to start with, and now they were full of water and very heavy.

Poor Donkey struggled home with the load of sponges. He was nearly dead with the weight of them.

'That just shows,' said his friend Barn-owl, when he told her about it, 'that if you try the same trick too often, you're sure to be found out.'

Too much cunning does us no good.

FOX AND STORK

Fox and Stork met one day beside the lake. Stork lifted his long beak out of the water and said, 'Good day'.

'Good day to you,' answered Fox with a low bow. 'And a very fine day it is. You're just the fellow I was looking for. Why not come along to my place this evening and have supper?'

'With pleasure,' answered Stork. 'I'll be with you at dusk.'

Now Reynard thought he would play a trick on Stork and make a fool of him. Then he could tell all the other animals about it, and show them what a clever fellow he was. He made some rich soup, and served it in two shallow dishes. He took one himself, and set the other in front of Stork.

'I think you'll enjoy this,' said Reynard, as soon as Stork was ready for supper. 'Don't wait, my dear Stork, or the soup will be cold.'

He licked his own supper up with much enjoyment, and watched poor Stork trying to drink from the shallow dish with his long thin beak. Of course Stork had almost no supper.

'Aren't you enjoying it?' asked Fox.

Stork answered that he wasn't feeling specially hungry, and had really enjoyed his supper immensely. Before he went, he asked Reynard to come to supper with him the following day.

'With the greatest
of pleasure!' answered Reynard.

Next evening, when Fox came to supper
with Stork, he found that once more the
meal was soup, and very good it smelt. But
Stork had served it in two tall jars with narrow necks. Stork dipped his long beak into
his jar, but Reynard got scarcely a drop
and had to be content with licking the top.
He was very angry indeed, and went home
without saying good night.

But afterwards Reynard saw that he had
been treated just as he deserved—and he
did *not* boast to the other animals of how
he had tricked Stork.

*Those who play tricks on others must expect
to be tricked themselves.*

JOAN

There was once a country girl called Joan. She worked hard at her old mother's dairy-farm, and very well she managed it. But Joan was a little vain—or, as people used to say, she gave herself airs. One evening she was walking back home through the meadows carrying a big can of milk on her head. She didn't hurry, for the evening was pleasant, and she liked to stroll along, turning things over in her mind.

'Let me see,' said Joan to herself, 'I shall get four or five shillings for this milk, and with that money I shall be able to get two dozen—no, three dozen eggs. That'll make three hundred, all told. Now if my three hundred eggs hatch out—well, I suppose some will turn out bad, and some will get taken by vermin—suppose I get two hundred and fifty young chicks. I'll sell them for pullets,' she went on. 'No, I'll keep them till they're full grown. Then poultry will be dear. Yes, I'll sell forty or fifty of them at least, and then I'll be able to go into town and buy myself a new dress. A silk dress it shall be. No, satin. I look best in satin. And what colour shall it be? Pink? No, not pink, nor yellow neither. *All* the girls are wearing yellow. I want to be different. White? No, not white: that Susan Huckaby always dresses in white, and I don't want to look a fright like *her*. Nasty, stuck-up thing! No, it shall be green—that's it. Green satin! I shall look a picture in green satin, and everyone will notice me.'

Joan smiled with happiness at the thought of everyone admiring her in the new dress she was going to buy. Then she went on, saying to herself:

'I shall wear it at the fair, so I will, and all the young fellows will want to dance with me. There'll be Tom, and Jack, and even that handsome Oliver that Susan is always running after. But I shan't have *one* of them. I shall just toss my head and have nothing to do with them. That's what I'll do—I'll toss my head!'

And here Joan was so taken up with her thoughts that she forgot all about the can of milk. She gave a haughty toss of her head, just for practice, and down fell the can, and all the milk was spilt in the grass. So poor Joan had to go home without anything to sell. The wonderful dream she had been enjoying all vanished like spilt milk.

Don't count your chickens before they are hatched.

CROW AND PITCHER

It was a very hot summer. There had been no rain for weeks. All the ponds and rivers were dry. Crow had spent a whole day looking for water. He flew here and there just for a beakful to quench his thirst. Not a drop could he find.

'Oh dear, oh dear!' thought Crow. 'If I don't have some water soon, I shall die.'

And it was true, for many of his brothers were already dead from thirst.

At last he noticed a pitcher standing in one corner of a yard. A housewife had been drawing water from the pump and had been called indoors. It was a heavy earthenware pitcher. Crow lighted on the edge of it and looked in. Yes, there was water in it. He stretched out his neck and reached down with his beak. The water was too low, but get some he must, or die.

Tired as he was, he hammered at the pitcher with his beak, trying to break it. But he had little strength, and the pitcher was too hard for him. Then he tried to knock it over. He stood on the ground and hit it with his wings; he ran against it, and flew against it, but it was no use. He could not knock it over.

At last, half dead with his efforts, he saw a heap of pebbles in another corner of the yard. He picked them up, one by one, and dropped them into the pitcher. He heard each one splash into the water, and then went back for more. It was as much as he could do to lift the pebbles and carry them across the yard.

Then at last there were so many in the pitcher that the water rose near enough to the top for him to be able to reach it with his beak. How greedily he drank! Of course he didn't get very much water, but it was enough to save his life.

Skill and patience achieve more than force.

ZORIAN THE STAR-GAZER

There was once an astronomer called Zorian, a very clever man with bright, thoughtful eyes and a long white beard. Every day he would read books about the sun, the moon and the other heavenly bodies; and at night he would gaze up at the stars and write down signs and figures on parchment scrolls. But it was not easy for Zorian to gaze at the stars from his house in the middle of the city, so on dark nights he used to walk out into the fields where he could get a better view.

One winter night, when there was not a cloud in the

sky, and no moon to dim the glittering of the stars, he wandered out of the town in a direction he had not taken before. He was making for a slight hill that lay not far off. As he went, he kept his bright eyes fixed on the planets overhead. So intent was he on his star-gazing that he strayed a little to one side of the path. Suddenly he lost his footing and toppled over the edge of a well. There was a great splash as he hit the icy water, and in a second he was up to his neck in it.

'Help!' cried Zorian as soon as he could get his breath. 'Come quickly, somebody, or I shall drown— or freeze to death! Help, help!'

As luck would have it, a soldier on his way back to town heard the astronomer's cries. Running to the well, he hauled the unfortunate Zorian out of the water, half dead with cold and fright. His teeth were chattering with cold and the icy water dripped from his beard.

They went back to the city together, and by the lighted window of a house the soldier recognized the man he had saved.

'Why, if it isn't the old fellow who roams about the streets with his eyes in the top of his head!' he exclaimed. 'If you ask my advice, sir, in future you'll forget about the stars and look where you're going.'

Zorian thanked the soldier for his help and went home.

Those who don't see what is in front of them run into danger.

THE TWO TRAVELLERS

It was getting dark. Two men were travelling through a wood to reach town before nightfall. They kept together for company. Soon there was a sound of heavy footsteps in the undergrowth, and suddenly a great brown bear stood in the pathway in front of them.

Without a thought for the other, the first traveller ran for the nearest tree and climbed high into the branches. As soon as he was safe, he looked down to see what was happening to his companion.

The second traveller ran too, but he tripped over a root and fell to the ground. He had no time to climb a tree, so he stayed where he was, pretending to be dead. He knew that bears will not touch a dead body. He kept as still as death, never moving a finger. His eyes were closed, and he scarcely dared to breathe.

The bear stooped down over him and nosed him all over. In particular, he sniffed at the traveller's face. But there was no sign of life in him, and soon the bear lumbered away into the woods and was seen no more.

As soon as he saw it was quite safe, the first traveller climbed down from his tree. The second traveller had got to his feet, and the first said to him:

'That was a close thing! I thought he had got you then. I'm glad you came to no harm, but tell me— what did the bear say to you when he put his nose to your ear? It looked to me as if he was whispering some secret.'

'That was no secret,' said the second traveller. 'He only told me to take care who I travel with, and not trust a man who runs away when his companion is in danger.'

So he left the first traveller and went on alone.

Avoid a companion who cannot be trusted.

KING LION IS ILL

One day Lion was ill, so very ill that he was too weak to come out of his den and hunt for food. He moaned and groaned, and a little bird, hopping about near the mouth of the den, heard him. So the bird flew through the jungle crying out, 'King Lion is ill! King Lion is ill!'

The other animals were sorry to hear this, and one by one they went to his den to visit him and say how sorry they were. Some of them took presents. Goat brought some herbs he had found on a hillside, and Antelope took some fruit he had gathered from the bushes.

Well, of course, when the animals came right into Lion's own den, he was able to fall upon them easily and kill them for his food. One by one, as each animal went in, he was put to death by clever King Lion and eaten. At last Reynard the Fox passed by the cave where the king was lying, and he called into the cave:

'Good day, Your Majesty, I trust you are beginning to feel better.'

'A little better, thank you,' answered Lion. 'Why did you not come sooner, like all my other subjects, to say how sorry you are that I have been ill?'

'I have only just heard the sad news,' said Reynard.

'Well, better late than never,' growled Lion. 'Come in, my dear fellow, and wish me good health.'

'Not just now, thank you,' said Fox slyly. 'Some other time, perhaps. I really ought to be getting home. I've just noticed something that tells me it would be extremely unwise for me to visit Your Majesty in his royal den.'

'And what is that, pray?' said Lion, somewhat annoyed.

'Well, you see,' said Reynard. 'I observe a number of footprints in the sand outside your den. Here is Goat's footprint, and here is Antelope's—and yes, here is Rabbit's, I think, and here is Donkey's.'

'What of it?' asked Lion. 'They have all had the good manners to come and bring me gifts. Naturally they left their footmarks outside.'

'Ah yes, Your Majesty,' said Reynard with a little

laugh, 'but you see, *all* the footprints point *into* your
cave. I see *none* coming *out*!'

So saying, Fox made a deep bow and vanished hastily
in the direction of his lair.

Cunning is defeated by greater cunning.

FARMER AND SONS

There was once an old farmer who had worked all his life growing grapes in his vineyard. He had done very well for his wife and their three sons. But at last it was near the time when he would die, and he wanted to teach his sons how to be good farmers. He wasn't at all sure that they really knew how important it is to work hard. So he called them to him one evening and said:

'My boys, it may be that I haven't much longer to live. But before I die, I want you to know that there is great treasure in my vineyard. Promise me you will remember that when I am gone.'

The three young men promised; and not long after that, their father died. Then they remembered what he had said, and began to look for the treasure he had left them in the vineyard. They pictured in their minds much coin, or silver plate, or things of that sort. How hard they worked in the hot sun, digging round the vines, turning over the soil with fork and spade, or going over every inch of ground with a hoe.

Well, the three brothers spent a month at least turning over the soil in that vineyard, but not so much as a penny piece could they find. At last they gave up, thinking their father must have been wandering in his mind. But soon the grapes began to appear, and although it was not a good year for other farmers, *their* grapes were bigger than any that had been grown before in that part of the country. When the grapes were ripe, how big and juicy they were! The brothers took them to the market, and were amazed at the high price they fetched. So now they understood what their father had meant by the great treasure he had left them in the vineyard. They saw that all their hard work had not been wasted, for it had made the grapes grow as they had never grown before.

Hard work brings prosperity.

7*a*

WOLF AND HOUSE-DOG

It was a cold night, and the full moon shone with a frosty glitter. Wolf was very, very hungry. He was lean and tired as he trotted through the woods with his tongue hanging out, ready to drop dead with misery and starvation. Presently up came House-dog and said 'Good evening'.

Wolf looked at House-dog and saw that he was fat and comfortable and well-fed. So he asked House-dog if he knew where he could find food.

'Oh, there's always food where I live,' answered House-dog. 'My master gives me plenty of scraps whenever I want them, and sometimes a big juicy bone.'

'Master?' said Wolf. 'What's that?'

'The man I live with,' said House-dog. 'I don't have to do much. Just scare away thieves in the night, and go out hunting when master wants to. It's a fine life. You ought to try it.'

Wolf didn't need to hear any more. The life of House-dog sounded so very comfortable and safe, and besides, he was so very, very hungry. So he trotted along beside House-dog to see if House-dog's master would take him in.

Then just as they came to the edge of the wood, and were getting near the village, Wolf noticed a mark on House-dog's neck. He stopped, and House-dog stopped too. Wolf pointed his paw at the mark.

'What's that?' asked Wolf.

'What's *what*?' said House-dog.

'That mark.'

'That? Oh, it's just a mark. I got it from the chain.'

'Chain?' said Wolf. 'Do you mean that your master puts a chain round your neck?'

'Sometimes,' said House-dog. 'I don't mind much. I'm used to it. Besides, he only chains me up sometimes. He always lets me out at night.'

'Never mind,' said Wolf. 'That's enough for me. You can keep your nice scraps and your bones and your hunting with master. But if ever I had a chain round *my* neck, I should die. I may be hungry, but at least I'm free. Good-bye, House-dog.'

And with that, Wolf turned round and went back into the woods, leaving House-dog to return home alone.

Freedom is better than comfort.

THE WOODCUTTER AND THE TREES

Matthew the Woodcutter needed a new handle for his axe. So he went into the great forest and said to all the trees:

'I have broken the handle of my axe, and have come to ask you for a new one. Will one of you give me a straight, sturdy piece of wood for what I need?'

The trees agreed to this small request, and the noblest of them put their heads together to decide which of all the trees in the forest should sacrifice itself to make Matthew a new handle for his axe.

'What about the pine?' said the oak. 'He is a good straight tree.'

'Not at all,' said the pine, who had overheard him. 'What about the elm?'

'I refuse,' said the elm. 'I would make a very poor handle. I tell you what, though. Let's make the ash surrender himself. He's a plain, homely little tree, and he can't very well object.'

So they made the ash give himself up to the woodcutter, and no sooner had Matthew made a new handle from the wood of the ash than he began laying about him in all directions. He cut down one tree after another, and all day long the forest rang with the noise of the blows.

'Alas!' said the oak to the cedar. 'Now I see what we have done. It will be our turn before long. He won't spare us. If only we hadn't sacrificed the poor ash, but stuck together and refused to give this wood-cutter the means to destroy us all!'

When great people sacrifice the poor and humble, they make trouble for themselves in the end.

WOLF AND GOAT

Wolf was roaming the green slopes at the foot of some craggy hills. He was hungry, and nowhere could he find any prey, for the goats that fed in those hills had learnt to keep well out of his way. Presently he spied a goat nibbling the grass among some rocks which were too steep and dangerous for any creature but a goat.

Wolf looked up and called out:

'Hi, Goat! What are you doing up there?'

'Eating my dinner,' answered Goat.

'What's the grass like?'

'Not bad,' said Goat.

'You ought to be careful,' called Wolf. 'You may miss your footing among all those loose stones. Then think what would happen to you. It's not safe.'

'Oh, I can manage all right,' said Goat, with his mouth full. 'I'm used to scrambling among the rocks.'

'Yes, but you should taste the grass down here,' Wolf went on. 'It's much sweeter and greener. Come on down and try it.'

'Thanks very much, Wolf dear,' answered Goat. 'But I think I'll stay where I am. You know, I have an idea it's *your* dinner you're thinking about—not mine!'

And he scrambled a little higher, just to be on the safe side, and went on with his nibbling.

Don't always trust those who say they want to help you.

COCK AND FOX

Chanticleer the Cock was perched on the farmyard fence. His red comb and his feathers shone in the sun, and he was very proud of himself as he gazed down upon his slaves, the hens. Just as he was telling himself for the twentieth time what a handsome fellow he was, Reynard the Fox came into the yard and caught sight of him.

'What a fine fat cock!' he said to himself. 'Now wouldn't he make a good dinner for me and my wife and the little ones? I wonder how I can get hold of him. I must be careful not to frighten him away.'

So the fox trotted carelessly towards Chanticleer and said:

'Good morning, my dear young fellow. I don't hear you singing today. Is anything the matter? I remember your father well. He was a wonderful singer. I bet you can't sing like him.'

'Much better,' answered Chanticleer boastfully. 'Just you listen to me.'

'Wait a moment,' said Reynard. 'Your late lamented father had a special way of singing. He used to shut his eyes tight, lift up his head and then start. Like that, he did it beautifully. I never heard anything so good in my life!'

'Then I will do the same,' said Chanticleer. 'If father did it, so can I.'

So saying, he stretched out his neck, took a deep breath and closed his eyes tightly. He was just going to begin crowing when Reynard gave a mighty spring and seized him by the throat. Then he ran swiftly out of the farmyard.

What a terrible shock for Chanticleer!

'Oh dear,' he said to himself, with his head hanging out of Reynard's jaws. 'Now I'm done for. How silly I was to listen to the fox's flattery!'

Reynard had to run hard, for the farmer and his men had seen him steal the cock and were now running after him with their rakes and hay-forks, shouting angrily.

'Drop that bird!' cried the farmer. 'You're a thieving rogue to steal my cock.'

'Mr. Fox,' said the cock in a thin little voice. 'Do you hear them shouting? Why don't you tell them that I belong to you now, not them?'

To Reynard this seemed a good idea. He stopped, turned round, and shouted to the farmer:

'This is *my* bird, you old fool, not yours!'

But as he opened his jaws to speak, Chanticleer slipped away and flew high into a tree out of reach. He was almost dead with fright, but he was safe. The fox ran away into the woods as fast as his legs could take him.

'What a fool I was to open my mouth!' he said, when he was safe at home. 'If I hadn't talked, I'd have been enjoying a good meal by now.'

And he determined to have more sense in future.

It is sometimes better to keep our mouths shut.

117

GOAT AND GOATHERD

A herd of goats was being driven slowly home to be milked. A boy was following them, trying to get them to move faster, as he wanted his supper. One goat strayed away from his companions to get at some fine long grass that grew a little distance from the path.

'Get back!' shouted the goatherd. 'Get back, there, I say!'

But Goat took no notice.

The boy called and whistled, but still Goat would not return to the herd.

At last the boy lost his patience and picked up a stone. He flung it at Goat, hoping to drive him back. But the stone struck one of Goat's horns and broke off the end of it.

'That's done it,' said the goatherd. 'Master won't half be angry with me if he knows I've been throwing stones at his animals.'

He ran up to Goat and spoke to him.

'Don't say anything about this, Goat,' he pleaded. 'Don't tell master, or he'll punish me. I didn't mean to hit you, only scare you a bit. I won't do it again.'

'That's all very well,' said Goat. 'But even if I say nothing, your master will see my broken horn. I'm afraid he's bound to find out.'

Facts speak louder than words.

TOM AND THE PITCHER

Tom knew where his mother kept the tall pitcher full of figs and nuts. When no one was in the kitchen, he lifted it down from the shelf and put it on the table. Then he pushed his hand into it and grabbed as many figs and nuts as he could hold. What a splendid feed he would have, and how he loved the green figs and the plump, ripe nuts!

But he had filled his hand so full that he couldn't get it out past the narrow neck. Try as he might, his bulging hand stuck fast, but he would not let go any of the figs and nuts.

'What a miserable boy I am!' said Tom, beginning to cry. 'It's not fair!'

'He began to wail so piteously that the serving-woman came in and asked what the matter was. Between his sobs Tom told her.

'Why, you greedy boy!' scolded the servant. 'If you weren't in such a hurry, you'd drop half the figs and not try to get so many at a time.'

Greed doesn't pay.

DONKEY, COCK, AND LION

Donkey and Cock lived together in a farmyard. Very contented they were, until one day King Lion came along. He looked at Donkey and saw that he was fat and healthy, so he thought he would make a meal of him.

Now there is one thing that King Lion is frightened of—and that is the crowing of a cock. Well, just as Lion was going to spring into the farmyard, it happened that Cock began to crow.

'Cock-a-doodle-do!' he cried, at the moment when Donkey first caught sight of King Lion. Lion, hearing the noise, stopped still, then turned away, and began to slink off.

'Fancy that!' cried Donkey. 'What a coward Lion must be to run away from the noise of a bird. I must be braver than Lion, for I hear Cock crow two or three times a day, and it doesn't scare *me* at all. Suppose I go and chase Lion myself! What fun it'll be to see him run off.'

So, laughing to himself, Donkey galloped out of the farmyard in the direction taken by King Lion. This time there was no cock-a-doodle to frighten Lion. So of course he turned on Donkey and sprang at him with a fierce growl. And that was the end of Donkey!

Pride and stupidity end in ruin.

INDEX OF FABLES